Study Guide for
I'M OK—YOU'RE OK

Study Guide for

I'M OK- YOU'RE OK

Richard Blackstock

Introduction by Thomas A. Harris
and Amy Harris

HARPER & ROW, PUBLISHERS

New York, Evanston, San Francisco, London

UNITY SCHOOL LIBRARY
UNITY VILLAGE, MISSOURI 64065

STUDY GUIDE FOR I'M OK—YOU'RE OK. Copyright © 1971 by Herald Publishing House. Introduction Copyright © 1974 by Thomas A. Harris. All rights reserved. Printed in the United States of America. No part of this book may be used or reproduced in any manner whatsoever without written permission except in the case of brief quotations embodied in critical articles and reviews. For information address Harper & Row, Publishers, Inc., 10 East 53rd Street, New York, N.Y. 10022. Published simultaneously in Canada by Fitzhenry & Whiteside Limited, Toronto.

ISBN: 0-06-060795-5

LIBRARY OF CONGRESS CATALOG CARD NUMBER: 73-20836

Designed by C. Linda Dingler

Contents

Introduction by Thomas A. Harris
  and Amy Harris — vii
Preface — xi
1. Freud, Penfield, and Berne — 1
2. Parent, Adult, and Child — 5
3. The Four Life Positions — 8
4. We Can Change — 12
5. Analyzing the Transaction — 16
6. How We Differ — 27
7. How We Use Time — 30
8. P-A-C and Marriage — 34
9. P-A-C and Children — 37

10.	P-A-C and Adolescents	42
11.	When Is Treatment Necessary?	45
12.	P-A-C and Moral Values	50
13.	Social Implications of P-A-C	55

Introduction

Paul Tournier begins his superb book *The Person Reborn** with this story:

"When I was quite a small boy, I used naïvely to dream of performing some great act.

"With my Meccano set I started building a mysterious machine, bristling with springs and gears. One day I was bold enough to tell my sister about my ambition. It was not going to be any ordinary machine, but one that would create life.

"Unfortunately my sister asked me to explain how it worked. I did not know what to say, and had to admit that I was depending on prayer: I would pray hard, and God would work a miracle by means of my machine!

*Harper & Row, 1966.

" 'In that case,' my sister exclaimed, 'what are all the gears for?' "

There is a similar question in the hearts of many Christian believers: If we have faith in God, do we really need assistance from psychological experts?

Most of us need all the help we can get, and some of the most needed help is in the form of information about how the mind operates to produce the actions and feelings we experience in our daily living.

It is a continuing revelation to receive validation for the information contained in *I'M OK—YOU'RE OK*. We have received many thousands of letters from readers. Many letters have been from Christians who have reported that their study of Transactional Analysis as presented in this book has produced dynamic insights into their relationships which have made them happier and more effective Christians, free to be innovative, warm and open to the Spirit of God in their lives. Many have asked, "Is there more material available about how to relate Transactional Analysis to the Christian Gospel?"

We are happy we now can respond *Yes* because of Richard Blackstock's excellent study guide. It is highly useful for personal as well as for group study. We are confident its use as a "gear" to the Gospel will lead to many hours of profound and practical discussion, shared experiences, and the stimulating discovery that God in fact "has not given us a spirit of fear, but of love and of power and of a sound mind."

> Thomas A. Harris, M.D., Author,
> *I'm OK—You're OK*
>
> Amy Harris, Co-Author, Chapter 12,
> "Moral Values and Religion"

Preface

I'm excited! *I'm OK—You're OK* is one of those *rare* books that has caused me to grow as a person. Because of its influence, I'm a different and, hopefully, a more Christian person in *my actual behavior*.

What's this book all about, you ask? This book is about you and me involved in the living of our lives—it deals with human beings and their problems.

What's the purpose of this book? The goal is to provide one more tool for persons desiring positive Christian growth.

How is this book relevant to my concerns as a Christian? If we see the scriptures in terms of personal *relationships,* then we also see this book as an aid in understanding and clarifying the scriptures and more important, *our* relationships with God and fellowmen.

Is "I'm OK—You're OK" a gimmick or a technique? No; however it could be misused in that manner. A more accurate description would be that it's a way of relating to others.

How can this book best be taught? We would be angry if the supermarket carried only one brand of everything. We like variety! So my suggestion would be to employ as many kinds of learning experiences as possible in the study of this book. This means the use of (1) role-playing, (2) occasional use of audio-visual aids, (3) sharing of class leadership with other class members. This material will become real, exciting, and meaningful only when it becomes *personal* to those in the class. This means that *everyone,* not just the teacher, is responsible for the success or failure of the class. If you are not familiar with role-playing, for example, but want to use it, ask someone else to help. One last suggestion: It is difficult to discuss this material if you or the class have not read it! Therefore suggest that they have a responsibility to read *if* they expect to learn!

May God richly bless your efforts to teach and to learn.

Study Guide for
I'M OK—YOU'RE OK

1. Freud, Penfield, and Berne

Introductory Statement

This chapter is designed to:
1. Acquaint the learner with current research and background information in the field of human behavior
2. Introduce the learner to the terms Transaction, Parent, Adult, and Child

Objective

The learner should be able to identify and use the term transaction and apply it to his own relationships with others.

Second, the learner should be familiar with and understand the four conclusions (p. 11, p.b.p. 32)*

---
*All p.b.p. numbers refer to the page numbers in the paperback edition.

of Penfield's research on the functioning of the brain.

Questions for Discussion

1. Harris states that the reason for this book is "not only the presentation of new data but also an answer to the question of why people do not live as good as they know how already" (p. 4, p.b.p. 24). Discuss with class what specific areas of growth *each member* would like to work on in this course of study.
2. Discuss the implications for our behavior as Christians considering the research of Penfield (p. 7, p.b.p. 27). Examples: FEELINGS + EXPERIENCES = TOTAL RECORDING IN BRAIN
   a. When you attend church services you feel unwanted, ignored, or "lost in the shuffle." Are you likely to continue coming? (FEELINGS + EXPERIENCES = *TOTAL* REALITY)
   b. You visit the home of a friend. He does not turn off the TV and is giving you only par-

tial attention. How do you feel? Do you want to stay?

c. You are enjoying the worship service—you feel uplifted by the prayers and testimonies. You want to attend these services often. Why? What does your *total* experience tell you?

3. God tells us through the scriptures to treasure up in our hearts and minds those good feelings and experiences. Harris lends support in conclusion No. 4 (p. 11, p.b.p. 32). Discuss.

4. Harris quotes Dr. Timothy Leary (p. 14, p.b.p. 35): "Of all the poetic notions and musical notes and lyric strains that we use, words like 'progress,' 'help,' and 'improvement' are the most far out. We operate with too little information about ourselves and about the other guy." Discuss the words we use in church that are similar in their ambiguity. Examples:

a. "Mr. Jones has repented and is ready for baptism."

b. "We sure had a good worship service last Sunday!"

c. "I feel I've made lots of spiritual growth this year."
5. *Note to teacher:* Emphasize this statement, "Parent is not the same as mother or father, Adult means something quite different from a grownup, and Child is not the same as a little person" (Harris, p. 15, p.b.p. 37).

2. Parent, Adult, and Child

Introductory Statement

In this chapter, the author gives us detailed descriptions and examples of the terms Parent, Adult, and Child.

Objective

The learner should be able to identify his own Parent, Adult, and Child and do the same with others in the group.

Questions for Discussion

1. Discuss Harris' definition of Parent, Adult, and Child. Give your own personal examples to illustrate.

2. How does the "Child" concept that Harris deals with differ (if it does) with that of Paul in the letter to the saints at Corinth (I Cor. 13:11)?
3. In regard to the parent, is the "Faith of Our Fathers" a parent admonition? Discuss.
4. Harris states that the Parent statements can't be erased (p. 20, p.b.p. 43). What implications will this have for our stewardship of parenthood?
5. As Harris suggests, it is only the *archaic, unthinking* use of the Parent that is inappropriate. Make a list of appropriate Parent responses and discuss with the class.
6. Harris believes there are other sources for Parent data besides the physical parents (p. 24, p.b.p. 48). One source he mentions is TV. What can parents do to "hook" the Adult in their children as they watch TV?
7. Discuss what "hooks your Child"—give examples. Have the class share their examples of the hooked Child.
8. Discuss the definition and examples of the Adult (p. 30, p.b.pp. 52, 53). How can church fellowship help to strengthen the person's Adult?

9. Make a list of your Parent, Adult, and Child statements used in a church, religious, or family context. Analyze the feeling (and the value) behind each statement.

3. The Four Life Positions

Introductory Statement

Purposes of this chapter include the following:
1. Acquaint the learner with the four life positions
2. Introduce the term "stroking" and its relationship to feelings
3. Define for the learner the "game" used in the P-A-C context
4. Explain the rationale behind the I'm OK—You're OK position and its consequences

Objective

The learner should be able to *identify and use* the following terms in the context of his own life situation: I'm not OK—You're OK, I'm not OK—You're not OK, I'm OK—You're not OK, I'm OK—You're OK, stroking, "game."

Questions for Discussion

1. Harris suggests that the young child decides "I'm not OK—You're OK." What kinds of behavior in the home lead the child to this conclusion? What are some specific behaviors that can minimize the not-OK feelings of our children?
2. Discuss the various types of stroking (physical and psychological) people want and need. What is the difference between stroking and "buttering up" someone? Stroking: to acknowledge the person's existence; i.e., shaking hands, "Hi, how are you?"
3. Harris quotes the psychologist Alfred Adler in reference to life's central problem (p. 42, p.b.p. 65). What scriptural support can you think of for this idea?
4. According to Harris, how the child sees himself in relation to his parents is vital to his growth (p. 42, p.b.p. 65). What kind of stew-

ardship implications does this have?

5. Discuss the four positions as outlined on p. 43 (p.b.p. 66) in terms of cause—what *causes* (behavior in terms of parent) a child to conclude one of the three nonverbal decisions?

6. Discuss life script as it relates to a position taken (I'm not OK—You're OK). Everything one says or does (life script) goes back to the cause—the position taken.

7. "However, once a position is decided, *all experience* is selectively interpreted to support it" (Harris, p. 47, p.b.p. 70). Relate this statement to the following examples:

   a. (Position) "I'm just not OK until I have my morning cup of coffee."
   b. (Position) "Mr. Jones is a fine person but he's not a member of the church."
   c. (Position) "When you can learn to be responsible then you can have the car."
   d. (Position) "I don't like you and I don't think you like me."
   e. (Position) "Men are selfish."
   f. (Position) "Women are sneaky."

8. Discuss the Christian implications of the I'm OK—You're OK position (pp. 50–53, p.b.pp. 74–77) in relation to the following:

a. Agency—the right to decide.
   b. Faith—the ability to move out in trust.
   c. Patience—willingness to wait to achieve desired goals.
   d. Perseverance—willingness to keep trying to achieve goals in spite of difficulties and obstacles.
   e. Risk-taking and the possibility of learning.
9. What price (what are the consequences) do you pay if you:
   a. play games (p. 51, p.b.p. 75)?
   b. take the position I'm OK—You're OK?

4. We Can Change

Introductory Statement

In this chapter (1) the learner is invited to use the P-A-C language to look at specific life situations and to identify Parent, Child, and Adult transactions. (2) The chapter deals with the motivation (values) behind change and when and why it occurs. (3) Harris states for the learner the goal of Transactional Analysis. Relate this goal (p. 58, p.b.p. 82) to the Christian concept of agency.

Objective

The learner should be able to use P-A-C language to look at his own transactions in the group, identify his values and motivation for positive change, relate the goal of Transactional Analysis to his understanding of the principle of agency.

Questions for Discussion

1. The first portion of chapter 4 talks about problem-solving in the context of three sets of data (Parent, Adult, and Child). Discuss specific problems the congregation has in its attempts to witness and worship for Christ in the context of P-A-C. What are the needs of the Parent (ideals), the Adult (realistic acceptance), and the Child (feelings) in each of us?
2. Harris states, "This is the fear—the archaic fear of the all-powerful Parent—which makes persons 'prejudge,' or which makes them prejudiced" (p. 57, p.b.p. 81). Let your Adult look at some of the specific prejudices you have in relation to church and Christian living (e.g., "People who come to church on Christmas and Easter are hypocrites").
3. Harris states that the goal of TA is "to enable a person to have freedom of choice, the freedom to change at will, to change the responses to recurring and new stimuli." Relate

this goal to the concept of agency. How can this goal be implemented in a congregation to enhance God's gift of agency?

4. How do you react to Harris' statement (p. 59, p.b.p. 83) that "restoration of the freedom to change is the goal of treatment"?

5. "When the Adult is in charge of the transaction, the outcome is not always predictable" (p. 60, p.b.p. 84). Give some examples of Christ demonstrating this situation (Luke 9: 49–50, 54–56, 59–60, 12:59).

6. Harris lists three possible situations that cause people to want to change (p. 60, p.b.p. 85). Does your Adult say which one (or all three) is the most appropriate for you? Which situation does the Christian hope for? Why?

7. "Does Man Have a Free Will" (p. 61, p.b.p. 86)? What do the scriptures say about man and his will?

8. Harris concludes the chapter by saying, "Thus we see the Adult as the place where the action is, where hope resides, and where change is possible" (p. 64, p.b.p. 88). Relate

this to scriptures that support this Adult functioning (Romans, chapter 7; Parable of the Prodigal Son, Luke 15:11–32—especially 15:17).

5. Analyzing the Transaction

Introductory Statement

The author in this chapter (1) gives us additional clues for the identification of the Parent, Adult, and Child. (2) He demonstrates by examples the Parent-Parent, Adult-Adult, and Child-Child transactions. (3) The author introduces the learner to Parent-Child, Child-Adult, and Adult-Parent transactions. (4) Harris illustrates the crossed transaction (and its consequences). (5) He invites us to consider *alternatives* for the Adult response and specific steps to help the learner strengthen his Adult once he has learned to recognize it.

Objective

The learner should be able to recognize and use Parent, Adult, and Child transactions in the group; identify crossed transactions in self and others in the group; be aware of possible *Adult alternatives* to crossed transactions.

Questions for Discussion

1. Discuss and *demonstrate* the Parent, Adult, and Child clues (physical and verbal, pp. 65–68, p.b.pp. 90–92).
2. Harris contends that "should" and "ought" can also be Adult words (p. 66, p.b.p. 90). How can we "check out" our own "oughts" and "shoulds" to see if they are appropriate for the situation at hand?
3. "This is because of the *good feeling* that comes from blaming and finding fault" (Harris, p. 69, p.b.p. 93). Since people are basically pleasure-seeking and pain-avoiding, how does the Adult in each of us deal with the "good feelings" of the blaming Parent?

4. Role-play (with volunteers) the situation with the two ladies on the bus (pp. 69–70, p.b.pp. 92–94). Act out the Parent-Parent *and* the Adult response possibilities.

5. Harris mentions (p. 70, p.b.p. 94) that "Someone who is enjoying a game of 'Ain't It Awful' does not welcome the intrusion of facts [Adult]." What price is Christ asking us to pay (daily) if we choose not to play games as a way of life?

6. Read through (verbally) and discuss illustrations on pp. 72–74 (p.b.pp. 97–98). Compare Adult-Adult, and Parent-Parent transactions.

7. Harris seems to be lending support to scripture when he says, "It's no fun to do *your* thing if everybody else is only interested in doing *his* thing" (p. 74, p.b.p. 99). Elaborate.

8. "A relationship between people cannot last very long without the Adult. Thus we may say that complementary Child-Child transactions exist with the permission and supervision of the Adult" (Harris, p. 76, p.b.p. 101) What are some indications (behavior) that tell us when a relationship is in trouble (without the Adult)?

9. Discuss and role-play the following transactions using Harris' first (p. 70, p.b.p. 95) and second (p. 81, p.b.p. 106) rules of communication:

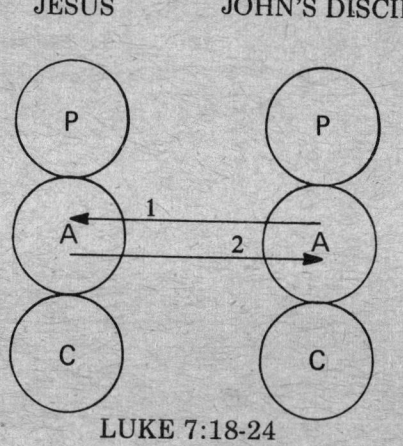

JESUS   JOHN'S DISCIPLE

LUKE 7:18-24

1. "Are you the one who was to come, or are we to look for someone else?"
2. "Go and tell John what you have seen and heard. The blind are recovering their sight, cripples are walking again, lepers being healed, the deaf hearing, dead men are being brought to life again, and the good news is

being given to those in need and happy is the man who never loses his faith in me."

Parent Responses (Possible)

2a. "Of course I am; you should never doubt my word."
2b. "What an obvious question—*really!*"
2c. "I wondered when you'd finally ask."

Possible Child Responses

2d. "Yes! I'm the one, I'm the *greatest!*"

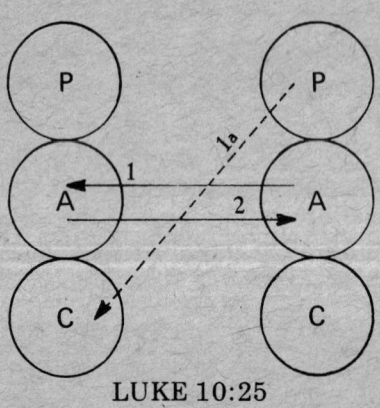

LUKE 10:25

1. "Master, what must I do to be sure of eternal life?"
1a. (Double message sent nonverbally) "I already know the answer but I'm going to corner you if I can."
2. "What does the Law say and what has your reading taught you?" said Jesus.

Possible Parent Responses

2a. "You should read and study the Law and obey your elders without question."
2b. "You're in need of a lot of repenting—go home and sorrow over your many sins."

Possible Child Responses

2c. "What are you trying to do—make a *fool* out of me?!"
2d. "Go away—I don't want to talk to you!"

JESUS   PILATE

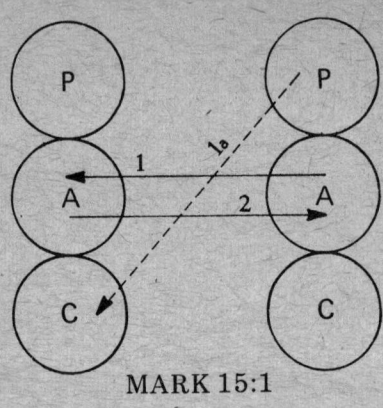

MARK 15:1

1. "Well, you—are you the king of the Jews?"
1a. (Double message) "You scrubby-looking man; you couldn't possibly be worth talking to."
2. "Yes, I am," he replied.

Possible Parent Responses

2a. "Who do you think you are—talking to *me* that way?"

2b. "If you would read the scriptures you would *know* I am!"

Possible Child Responses

2c. "Not only am I king of the Jews but *your* king too!"
2d. Silence, followed by crying.

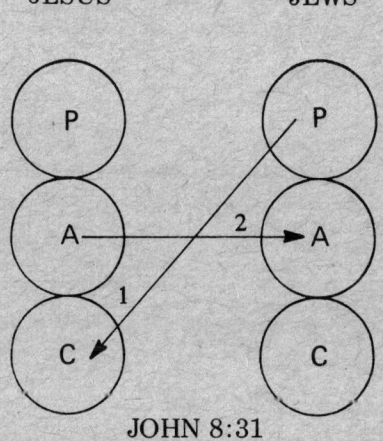

JOHN 8:31

1. "How right we are," retorted the Jews, "in calling you a Samaritan, and mad at that!"
2. "No," replied Jesus, "I am not mad. I am

honoring my Father, and you are trying to dishonor me. But I am not concerned with my own glory: there is one whose concern it is, and he is the true Judge. Believe me when I tell you that if anybody accepts my words, he will never see death at all."

Possible Parent Responses

2a. "It's *you* who are mad! I've shared the truth with you and *you've* rejected it! And the condemnation is on *your* heads!"
2b. "How many times have I told you—I'm not a Samaritan, I'm a Jew—like you!"

Possible Child Responses

2c. "I don't care what you say to me—*my* way is better!"
2d. "You're making me angry—I'm going to get you if you don't stop saying that!"
10. "The first way, therefore, to build the strength of the Adult is to become sensitive to Parent and Child signals. Aroused feelings

are a clue that the Child has been hooked. To know one's own Child, to be sensitive to one's own NOT OK feelings, is the first requirement for Adult data processing" (Harris, p. 92, p.b.p. 118). Have each member of the class make a list of Parent and Child information as an assignment. Discuss and compare the various lists. How are they alike? How do they differ? How can we update these lists? Apply Adult questions (p. 93, p.b.p. 118) to the lists.

1. "We fear the Parent in others; their Child we can love" (Harris, p. 93, p.b.p. 119). Demonstrate this by each member in the group sharing an experience of joy. How do we respond to that sharing? How do we respond to admonishing and commanding (Parent)?

2. "Another way to strengthen the Adult is to take the time to make some big decisions about basic values, which will make a lot of smaller decisions unnecessary" (Harris, p. 94, p.b.pp. 119, 120). What priorities (e.g., persons are important) does the Christian have for his basic values as they are *demonstrated* in behavior?

3. "This kind of giving [Adult] can be a chosen

way of life" (Harris, p. 95, p.b.p. 121). How can you show your family you have *chosen* the Christian (Adult) way of life? Can it be done best by preaching? admonishing? showing? demonstrating? What method is believed?

14. Ask the class to conduct an experiment. *Discuss and use* the six ways of strengthening the Adult (pp. 95–96, p.b.pp. 121, 122). Ask them to use the six ways in their behavior for one week and report the results at the next class meeting.

5. How We Differ

Introductory Statement

This chapter points to the specific ways we differ from the perspective of P-A-C. Harris introduces us to terms such as contamination, exclusion, decommissioned Adult.

Objective

The learner should be able to identify his own prejudices by examination of Parent data; identify through example and paraphrasing these terms: contamination, exclusion, decommissioned Adult.

Questions for Discussion

1. "Prejudice develops in early childhood when the door of inquiry is shut on certain subjects by the security-giving parents. The little person dares not open it for fear of parental rebuke" (Harris, p. 98, p.b.pp. 124, 125). Think of some ways your children developed certain prejudices about church, Christianity, people, etc. through their association with you. In our society prejudice usually has a negative connotation. Discuss some prejudices that are helpful and OK.

2. "The only ways to eliminate prejudice are [1] to uncover the fact that it is no longer dangerous to disagree with one's parents and [2] to update the Parent with data from today's reality" (Harris, p. 99, p.b.p. 125). Apply this information to some prejudice you have which has arisen from a defensive attitude. Role-play if possible.

3. "Typical of the Parent-Contaminated Adult with a Blocked-Out Child is the man who is duty-dominated, always working late at the

office, all business, impatient with family members who want to plan a skiing trip or a picnic in the woods" (Harris, p. 100, p.b.p. 127). Which one of the New Testament apostles fits this description? (See John 12:1–8).

4. Harris suggests (p. 103, p.b.p. 129) that: "One way to determine whether or not a person has a Parent is to determine the existence of feelings of shame, remorse, embarrassment, or guilt." How can the Good News of Jesus Christ help us to know what is legitimate (appropriate) guilt, shame, or embarrassment?

5. Harris, throughout this chapter, stresses the fact that inconsistent behavior on the part of parents causes many difficulties for the child and his OK-ness. How can the Christian parent who wants the best environment for growth for his family (and himself) use P-A-C for this purpose?

6. Harris defines health in terms of an emancipated Adult (p. 113, p.b.p. 140). If we tentatively accept this definition as true, what implications does it have for the Christian in family life? congregational activities? marriage relationships? work?

7. How We Use Time

Introductory Statement

In this chapter the author discusses with us the six types of experience—ways we use our time. More important, Harris illustrates some of the *consequences* of our use of time.

Objective

The learner should be able to identify and use the six time structures to examine his own use of time.

Questions for Discussion

1. Harris suggests (p. 115, p.b.p. 142) that all of us try to achieve programming or structuring of time. Give specific examples of this structuring in your church and home life. Can you see where some of this structuring is an outgrowth for recognition of self? Discuss.
2. Discuss scriptures that deal with time and our use of it.
3. Under which category of the six types of experience (p. 115, p.b.p. 142) do the following fall?
   a. Watching TV
   b. Home visiting
   c. Communion Service
   d. Talking in the foyer after church
4. How may a person experience withdrawal (pp. 115–116, p.b.pp. 142, 143) during a preaching service or a prayer service? How can you tell if a person has withdrawn?
5. Discuss specific rituals used at church functions, home, and at work.
6. What is the purpose of a ritual (p. 116, p.b.p.

143)? Is a ritual necessarily "good" or "bad"? Discuss.

7. Discuss the advantages of activity-oriented behavior. Next, the disadvantages!

8. Name some ways you engage in pastimes (spend passing time).

9. What is the price (consequences) if you play games as a way of life (games as defined on page 120, p.b.p. 147)?

10. What price (consequences) do you pay if you decide to act out of the "I'm OK—You're OK" position?

11. Ask for volunteers to act out (role-play) the "Yes—But" script on pages 120–121 (p.b.pp. 148, 149). Discuss how the Adult might be hooked instead of continuing the game–playing.

12. What is the danger of being aware of others playing "games" and calling it to their attention?

13. How may P-A-C become a tool for the manipulation of others?

14. What specific responsibility does your congregation, and you as a person, have in providing the "I'm OK—You're OK" atmos-

phere? What benefits would this provide?
15. Discuss the question dealing with the six types of time used (p. 125, p.b.pp. 152, 153) in terms of appropriateness and dominance.

8. P-A-C and Marriage

Introductory Statement

Harris, in this chapter, looks at the marriage relationship using P-A-C as a perspective. He examines some problems basic to every marriage and suggests some alternative resolutions to those problems.

Objective

The learner should be able to apply P-A-C language to his own marriage relationship (if he's married) and use his Adult to see alternative solutions to his marriage situation.

Questions for Discussion

1. What specific items would be included in Harris' statement concerning "archaic data which each partner brings to the marriage" (p. 127, p.b.p. 155)?
2. How do the marriage vows help both partners to bring the Adult into the marriage contract? recognize and provide for the needs of the Child of each partner?
3. "Fortunate and rare are the young partners whose Parent contains the impressions of what a good marriage is" (Harris p. 127, p.b.p. 155). Define a "good marriage" in terms of the Child, the Parent, the Adult.
4. Name some specific steps that can be taken to strengthen the Adult of your children in regard to marriage and its expectations.
5. "Although a Jewish man may agree in advance that his children be raised in the Catholic faith according to the wishes of the Catholic bride-to-be, this does not mean that he may not be deeply troubled about it later on" (Harris, p. 132, p.b.p.160). Change the Jew-

ish man to your own faith; discuss with the class what his Adult must consider in light of his Parent and Child data.

6. "This is not to say that we cannot hold to the ideal of marriage as a permanent bond, but we must not see it as a license to trap people into an arrangement in which they forever are bound by legal but no moral obligations" (Harris, p. 133, p.b.p. 161). Use your Adult and discuss the "moral obligations" that bind a good marriage together.

7. Harris discusses the need for partners in marriage to look with the Adult at the present realities of their marriage situation (p. 141, p.b.p. 169). How can the married members of the congregation witness to our young people the validity of Adult-established goals?

8. Discuss the questions found on page 142 (p.b.p. 171) concerning the values important to the marriage relationship. Add your own questions to this list. Is it possible to suggest that everyone will agree with the priority of values you've chosen even if they represent your best thinking? Discuss.

9. P-A-C and Children

Introductory Statement

Seeing the development of children through P-A-C is the topic of this chapter. Harris emphasizes the key role of *parents* in changing the nature of the parent-child relationship. Once *parents* take the initial responsibility to change *then* the behavior of the Child begins to change.

Objective

The learner (if a parent) should be able to identify and apply P-A-C language to his transactions with his own children.

Questions for Discussion

1. What are the implications for family life and family ministry in light of Harris' belief that "to help children is to help parents"?
2. What do the scriptures say in support of Harris about the relationship of parent and child? (See Eph. 6:1–4, Prov. 22:6, Prov. 29:15, Eccles. 4:13.)
3. Harris mentions the problem children and adults of today have—that of "sorting out what is fact and what is fiction." What do the scriptures tell us to do with this problem? (Isa. 1:16–18.)
4. Discuss the advantages and disadvantages of the P-A-C expectant-parent classes. Are they necessary in your way of thinking? Why or why not?
5. Discuss these scriptures in light of Harris' statement that "when mother's Child gets hooked and she gets involved in a Child-Child slugfest with Junior, he senses his world is in bad shape indeed" (p. 154, p.b.p. 182). (I Cor. 13:11, I Cor. 14:20.)

6. "Demonstrating what an Adult is is far more effective than defining what an Adult is!" (pp. 154–155, p.b.p. 183). Discuss the importance of modeling Adult behavior as a responsibility of the parents.
7. Harris (p. 155, p.b.p. 183) mentions some dangers. Discuss these in relation to the following scriptures: Eph. 6:1-4, Prov. 22:6, Prov. 29:15, Eccles. 4:13.
8. Harris states that agency (choice) is the basis for behavior (p. 156, p.b.p. 184). "The choice is one of being consistently helpful to the small child or beating him down and back into catastrophic terror with the bellowing of the archaic Parent, a product of countless generations of parental self-righteousness." Is this choice related to Jesus' invitation "to daily take up your cross (choice-making) and follow me"? Discuss.
9. Discuss the *two jobs* parents have when difficulties arise in the home with children (p. 156, p.b.p. 185).
10. "A transaction particularly disorganizing to a youngster is one in which the parent, in answer to a request by the youngster, tediously gives *all* the reasons why he shouldn't

do something instead of simply stating the *main reason*. If that main reason isn't robust enough to be stated in simple terms, then perhaps it should be rejected" (p. 157, p.b.p. 186). Discuss, citing examples from your own experience.

11. "The really urgent aspect of this situation [not OK] is that all of life is competitive, beginning with life in the family and extending through all of school and into the grownup world of life in society" (p. 160, p.b.p. 188). What can church fellowship do to help, in specific terms? Discuss.

12. Discuss the following statement in relation to church, home, and school settings: "The Parent [in each of us] says, 'Do More.' The Adult asks, 'Do *what* more?'" (p. 160, p.b.p. 189). Example: Work harder on your homework without specifying a particular thing to improve performance.

13. Harris says, "P-A-C could well be the most important thing we can do to solve the problems which beset us and threaten to destroy us" (p. 161, p.b.p. 190). What does your Parent say in response? What does your Child say? Your Adult?

14. "We have to examine our absolutes. Is complete honesty always the best? It would seem to be. However, as Trueblood points out, 'We are always guilty of oversimplification when we stress only one of several relevant principles'" (p. 166, p.b.p. 195). How is your Parent responding to this statement? Your Child? Your Adult? Discuss.
15. Harris states (p. 169, p.b.p. 198), "It is not possible to teach nonviolence with violence." Statements by Jesus support this: Matthew 26:49–50, Luke 6:27–29. Discuss the implications for family life.

10. P-A-C and Adolescents

Introductory Statement

Harris, in this chapter, emphasizes the primary need for *adequate and accurate communication* between parents and their teen-age children. P-A-C provides this common language for better communication about mutual concerns. The author also uses P-A-C as a tool for developing value structure for adolescents based upon the worth of persons as a priority.

Objective

The learner (if a parent) should be able to use P-A-C language to identify and discuss problems of mutual concern to teen-age children.

Questions for Discussion

1. Harris makes a point that adolescents in our society face a dilemma (p. 176, p.b.p. 206). Discuss with this statement in mind: "The Adult does not develop under these circumstances" (p. 176, p.b.p. 206).
2. "The central difficulty is that he and his parents often are still working under the terms of the old Parent-Child contract" (p. 177, p.b.p. 207). Discuss the specifics of the Parent-Child contract you grew up under. How does this differ from what you expect as the parent? Use your *Adult* to process this question!
3. Relate the scripture, "Parents, provoke not your children to anger," to the Parent-Child contract.
4. How can the Adult-Adult contract be obtained (p. 180, p.b.p. 210)?
5. Harris mentions the helpful part of the Parent information that every teen-ager needs (p. 182, p.b.p. 212). Discuss in specific detail: values, realities, the importance of people,

and his own worth. Are these taught or caught?

6. In his discussion of sex outside marriage, Harris states, "The Adult view can be quite different as it asks the question, 'What does this do to persons?' " What does the Parent say? the Child?

7. If we consider that *our own behavior* teaches our children, what is the best insurance for their OK feelings about self and sex (pp. 184–185, p.b.pp. 214, 215)?

8. Discuss the value of sharing (an Adult function) the information found in the last paragraph on page 184, p.b.p. 215 with our teenage sons and daughters. *Under what circumstances* will they seriously consider its value for them? What are some possible reasons for their choosing to disregard its counsel?

9. Discuss the key questions (p. 193, p.b.p. 224) the Adult asks relative to *any* behavior being considered.

11. When Is Treatment Necessary?

Introductory Statement

This chapter is devoted to sharing with the learner some of the motivations behind the behavior of each of us. It points us to a sense of *hope* that we can become "in charge" of ourselves if we *choose* to do so. It is not left to chance or "that's just the way I am and can't change."

Objective

The learner should be able to identify some of his own motivations for behavior, be aware of the *hope* of "I can change!" as a philosophy of life, sense the invitation to be "in charge" of himself.

Questions for Discussion

1. "For some people, however, the Adult is impaired to the point where they cannot function. They are crippled by repetitious failure or immobilized by guilt" (Harris, p. 196, p.b.p. 228). Discuss *specific kinds* of repetitious failures and guilt feelings that immobilize. What are some physical symptoms of this kind of behavior?

2. "The goal is to make every person in treatment an expert in analyzing his own transactions" (Harris, p. 197, p.b.p. 229). Relate this to the scripture, "Let *each man examine himself*—as to his worthiness" (I Cor. 11:28) and "Each man must work out his own salvation" (Phil. 2:12).

3. Harris, on page 198 (p.b.p. 230), stresses the importance of one human being helping another human being help himself. How is this similar (or different) from the personal ministry of Jesus?

4. Harris talks (p. 199, p.b.p. 231) about a "contract." How is his suggested contract much

like a baptismal convenant or contract? Discuss how the goals of both contracts are alike, different.

5. "People can recover from the symptoms of mental illness, but they don't recover from a label" (Menninger, p. 199, p.b.p. 231). What kind of labels do you use to label people? Are they harmful to the person being labeled? How do you know if they are harmful or not? What are some accurate ways of "checking it out"?

6. "Words that obscure the truth must be discarded for those that say it simply, accurately, and directly; and truth about how we are put together, in large measure, is what makes us free" (Harris, p. 200, p.b.p. 232). What are some words that obscure the truth for you? What other words would say it more effectively for you?

7. Compare and discuss the following responses to the question, "What am I, anyway?" (p. 200, p.b.p. 232) Which response is behavior-oriented? Is one response (or the other) necessarily good or bad, right or wrong? What are the advantages and disadvantages of statement "a"? of statement "b"?

    a. "You are a Christian and a child of God."
    b. "You have a lot of not OK in your Child with a fairly sizable contamination of your Adult, which lets you come on inappropriately at times and gives your hovering Parent an opportunity to beat on your Child."
8. Harris, page 201 (p.b.p. 233), says that there has been an implication that it takes a long time to change. However, Harris says the amount of time largely depends on the person and his *willingness* to change. What does Christ say about change and how long it will take? In Matthew 8:19–22 Christ asks us to respond *now*—not to put off serving Him. In Luke 19:1–10 we are asked to receive Christ now.
9. "Treatment is speeded only by keeping the Adult in charge. Only the Adult can spot the Child or the Parent" (Harris, p. 203, p.b.p. 235). Relate this to Jesus' statement concerning what we will say in his behalf (Matthew 10:17). *Note:* Jesus says, "Don't worry about coming across Child or Parent; wait and let Adult function." Discuss the possibility of one of the functions of the Holy Spirit being

discernment (awareness) of the Parent or the Child by the Adult.

10. "We are surrounded by a sense of urgency to help people in trouble, many people in trouble" (Harris, p. 204, p.b.p. 238). Discuss *in specific detail* how a Christian using P-A-C can be of help to people wherever he finds them or himself.

11. "We cannot, after all, resign from the human race, game-ridden as it may be. If we are not to be overcome by evil, then we must overcome evil with good. This we cannot do if we withdraw from all the relationships in which games exist" (Harris, p. 211, p.b.p. 244). Discuss *in specific detail* how the Adult decides *which* choice is appropriate, based upon Christian values.

12. P-A-C and Moral Values

Introductory Statement

Harris deals with a central problem that each of us faces. Constructing a value system using P-A-C and the ultimate worth of persons is the theme of this chapter. Harris also looks at Christianity through the perspective of P-A-C. He challenges us to update our religious experience in light of P-A-C. He sees healthy religious experience as Adult, as opposed to Parent.

Objective

The learner should be able to construct a list of his own values and their priority, discuss the relationship between P-A-C and Christianity, examine our religious experiences in terms of P-A-C.

Questions for Discussion

1. Choose one or more of the questions on pages 213–214 (p.b.pp. 246, 247) as a lead-off discussion of the chapter.
2. In what ways does *your* reality differ from that of any other Christian (p. 214, p.b.p. 247)?
3. "One such reality is the need for and existence of a system of moral values." How have you developed your system of moral values? What part did each institution play in the formation of your value system? Can you recognize the Parent, Adult, and Child portions of your value system (p. 215, p.b.p. 248)?
4. What can Christianity contribute to the world of science through providing a moral value system? Can scientific investigation help the Christian to be more aware of his human situation?

5. How does Jesus' command to "love one another as I have loved you" differ from the Golden Rule (in light of Harris' statement on page 216, p.b.pp. 249, 250)?
6. What Parent data is reliable and worthy of passing on to young children (p. 217, p.b.pp. 250–251)?
7. The current term for expressing subjective values is "Doing your own thing." What primary values are important for all men as Adults regardless of their culture (p. 218, p.b.p. 251)?
8. What are some practical implications for your life if the position taken is, "Persons are important" ("Worth of Persons," p. 220, p.b.p. 254)?
9. (P. 225, p.b.p. 259) What scripture can you recall that illustrates Harris' quote of Paul Tillich, "Before sin is an act, it is a state"? Relate this to the idea that before games were played, a position was taken (Gen. 4:1–8, Ezek. 38:10–11).
10. (P. 226, p.b.p. 260) Consider specific Parent institutional statements that might have led a certain leader of your church to his religious convictions. How did he use his Adult to look

at the current religious scene? Discuss.
11. Consider which aspects of the church are Parent, Adult, and Child in terms of ordinances, sacraments, types of services, etc. Discuss.
12. Harris states (p. 228, p.b.p. 262), "It is the *position* which we must 'confess' or acknowledge or comprehend." What is this position in *simple specific terms?*
13. Respond to Harris' statement that "confession [acknowledgment of a position] without change is a game." How can you prevent game-playing in your life? Discuss.
14. Harris believes that Christ's message of grace has been distorted in our culture to fit our game patterns. Give some specific examples of how that distortion may have occurred.
15. (P. 229, p.b.p. 264) In what specific ways is your congregation a "repository of parent dictates designed to keep things as they are"? Harris contends this is OK, but hardly enough considering the conditions in the world. Discuss. In what specific ways is your congregation advocating and demonstrating change that will significantly affect persons?
16. "The contract is that *we* [the members of the

congregation] *don't really have to change; after all, we are such nice people*" (p. 230, p.b.p. 264). To what degree is this statement true for you (specifically)?
17. (P. 230, p.b.p. 264) Harris suggests that some people have left the church because of all the "inconsistency and hypocrisy." How can we "hook" their Adult and invite them to fellowship with us again?

13. Social Implications of P-A-C

Introductory Statement

In this chapter the author applies the principles of P-A-C to the relationships of (1) nation to nation (foreign policy), (2) individual morality, and (3) child rearing. The central theme of the chapter seems to be: Change for the better is possible when the *Adult* is in charge. That is the goal and the hope of this study.

Objective

The learner should be able to analyze current events in terms of P-A-C, examine and identify his personal morality using P-A-C language.

Questions for Discussion

1. (P. 245, p.b.p. 280) Harris suggests that we become as careful in examining our existing institutions as we are with individuals. What kind of framework (questions) can we use to examine the bearers of Parent information (institutions)?

   "These questions, with variations and modifications, may be used as the basis for examining any system (e.g. the home, the government, mathematics, historical description, war, marriage, astrophysics, the school, suburbia, the draft, etc.).
   What are the purposes of the system?
   What roles are people assigned?
   What rules must be followed?
   What rights and restrictions are given and imposed?
   What are some of its critical, underlying assumptions?
   What are its key words?
   To what extent do the problems of the

system require decisions? choices? solutions?

To what extent is the system changing?

What are the mechanisms for change within the system?

To what extent is the language of the system obsolete?

What are the critical, nonverbal symbols of the system?

To what extent are these changing?

What is the actual effect of the system on people?

To what extent is this different from the ostensible purpose of the system?

Are there alternatives to the system? Can we do without it?

How is the system related to other systems of knowing and behaving?"

—From *Teaching as a Subversive Activity,* by Neil Postman & Charles Weingartner, Delacorte Press: New York, 1969, p. 120

2. Harris states (p. 251, p.b.p. 287), "Not all automatic responses to authority are good."

Think of some automatic responses to authority you use that could be questioned by others. Discuss.

3. The author reminds us that "Decisions made by the Adult do not guarantee acclaim, popularity, or safety, particularly among those who are too threatened by reality to take a second look at it." Is this the same kind of life-style Jesus demands of us? Discuss. ("He who would save his life must be willing to lose it in my cause.")

4. (P. 256, p.b.p. 291) "Dialogue, if it is to get us anywhere, must be based on agreement of what to examine and an agreement on the words to describe what we observe." What does this say to the format or structure of church school classes? How might Adult-Adult communication be enhanced and nurtured? Discuss.

5. Harris implies (p. 256, p.b.p. 292) that the possibility for change is evident because we can *choose* not to respond with the Child but with the Adult. Relate this to scripture. Discuss.